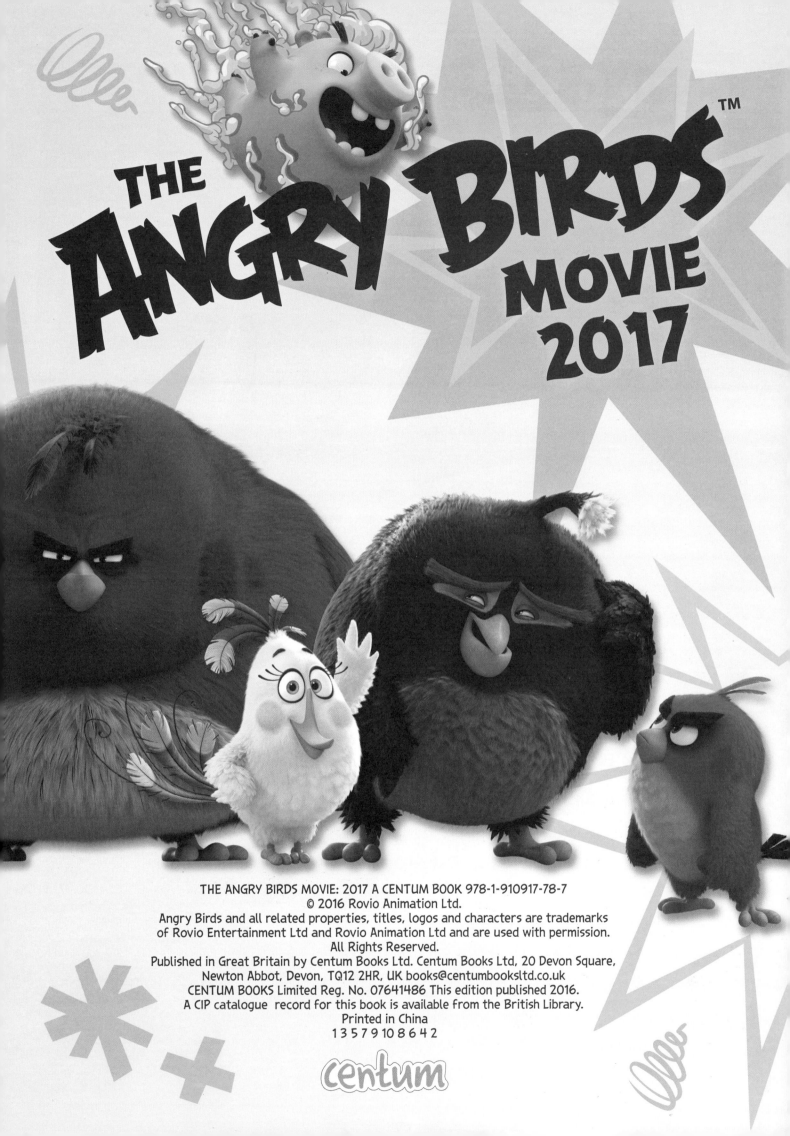

THE ANGRY BIRDS MOVIE
2017

THE ANGRY BIRDS MOVIE: 2017 A CENTUM BOOK 978-1-910917-78-7
© 2016 Rovio Animation Ltd.

Published in Great Britain by Centum Books Ltd. Centum Books Ltd, 20 Devon Square,
Newton Abbot, Devon, TQ12 2HR, UK books@centumbooksltd.co.uk
CENTUM BOOKS Limited Reg. No. 07641486 This edition published 2016.
A CIP catalogue record for this book is available from the British Library.
Printed in China
1 3 5 7 9 10 8 6 4 2

centum

SEEING RED

Everything you needed to know about Bird Island's unlikely hero!

NAME: RED

ABOUT: Red is Bird Island's angriest resident. But he's equally as angry as he is brave (meaning he's very brave!) and takes each and every challenge head on!

LIVES: On his own in a hut away from the rest of town. He likes his own company.

FRIENDS: Chuck and Bomb are his closest friends, but he also sometimes hangs out with Matilda and Terence.

MOVIE PREVIEW: Red's life couldn't get any worse, until the pigs arrived!

Meet the angriest member of the flock.

Red loves his house more than anything.

He's not a fan of hugs.

CHASING CHUCK

Blink and you'll miss him!

Chuck is one of the friendliest birds around!

NAME: CHUCK

ABOUT: Chuck is so fast he can do things without his friends even noticing. He may not be the brightest beak in the flock, but he's loyal and always tries to do his best.

FRIENDS: Chuck is friends with everyone. But his best buds are by far Red and Bomb.

MOVIE PREVIEW: Chuck uses his awesome speed to pull off some amazing tricks. Plus, he's pretty great at yoga, too!

Chuck loves his new Anger Management friends!

He's had a few brushes with the law for his speedy ways.

7

BOOM, HERE'S BOMB!

Don't make him angry... he might blow his top!

Never throw him
a surprise party.

Bomb is really sweet despite
his IED (Intermittent Explosive Disorder).

He enjoys learning new things,
even yoga!

NAME: BOMB

ABOUT: You won't be surprised to find out that Bomb explodes. He's large, strong and a real asset to the flock.

FRIENDS: Bomb tries to be friendly with most birds, but he gets on well with those who understand him – like the rest of the Anger Management Class.

MOVIE PREVIEW: It's a daily struggle, but Bomb has to learn how to control his explosive talents. Luckily his unique ability is going to become very useful!

MEDITATING MATILDA!

Keep calm and carry on meditating.

NAME: MATILDA

ABOUT: She runs the Anger Management Classes on Bird Island. She's all about meditation and staying calm at all times.

FRIENDS: She's so calm and warm that most of Bird Island are in awe of her. In fact, there isn't a bird who doesn't like her.

MOVIE PREVIEW: Matilda tries to help her class deal with their anger issues, but maybe she has some of her own?

Matilda knows every yoga pose there is.

Matilda loves helping those Angry Birds!

She's a master of meditation.

THE PESKY PIGS

They come in peace.
No honestly, they do!
Well... okay, they don't.
They might actually have a plan
up their sleeves...

Leonard is the bearded leader of the pigs.

Poor Red – the pigs have invaded his quiet beach!

NAMES: LEONARD

BIGGEST AMBITION: Stealing eggs and building suspiciously bad constructions to hide them in.

FRIENDS: Other pigs!

MOVIE PREVIEW: When the pigs first arrive on Bird Island, most of the flock can't wait to make friends. Fortunately, one crimson crusader suspects foul play and is going to stop at nothing to reveal the pigs' true nature.

FIVE TAIL-CURLING FACTS:

The pigs aren't very clever, even though they manage to outsmart the birds at first!

They aren't really afraid of any bird, apart from the big, silent one!

They come to the island knowing exactly what they are going to find there.

They are the ones who teach the birds how to fly using a slingshot.

Their favourite food is, unfortunately, eggs!

How many piggies are having fun on these two pages? Who is your favourite?

BIRD ISLAND

Get to know the rest of the flock!

NAME: STELLA

TOP TRAIT: Seeing the good in everyone she meets.

FRIENDS: Stella has many friends. She's the bird other birds want to be.

MOVIE PREVIEW: Stella wants to believe the pigs are her friends. Is she going to be disappointed?

Stella loves the spotlight!

His favourite word is "Grr!"

NAME: TERENCE

TOP TRAIT: He's big. Very big.

FRIENDS: Terence also has a bit of a soft spot for Matilda.

MOVIE PREVIEW: He may be the strong, silent type, but when it comes to the crunch - the birds are happy Terence is on their side.

Don't mess with the Judge!

NAME: JUDGE PECKINPAH

TOP TRAIT: The ability to misread most situations and make lots of wrong decisions.

FRIENDS: Cyrus. Without him he'd be half the bird (literally).

MOVIE PREVIEW: The judge is the bird responsible for sending Red to Anger Management, as well as welcoming the pigs to Bird Island. So he has a LOT to answer for.

NAME: MIGHTY EAGLE

TOP TRAIT: Mighty Eagle is very large and very strong. When summoned, he can use his immense strength to clear any pigs in his wake. Or so he thinks!

FRIENDS: Why would any bird be his enemy?

MOVIE PREVIEW: Part myth, part legend, Mighty Eagle lives alone on the mountainside. Will Red be able to convince him to help defeat the pigs?

There's nothing Mighty Eagle loves more than himself.

ANGRY BIRDS PART ONE:
A disturbance on the beach!

This is the story of a bird. A pretty normal, average, everyday bird. You know, the kind of bird that doesn't fly and lives far away from the rest of the flock on the beach. Just a normal, average, everyday bird with one small problem. He gets angry. **Very, very angry**.

Now, this isn't really a problem for Red. In fact, he secretly enjoys letting off a bit of steam – whether it's kicking a sign or slamming a door, being angry feels good!

The trouble is, not everyone on Bird Island agrees with Red. In fact, if it was up to Judge Peckinpah, everyone in the flock would be calm, happy and annoyingly upbeat 365 days a year. That's why, when Red caused chaos at a young hatchling's party, Red was ordered to attend Anger Management Classes – held by Matilda.

Things didn't get off to the best start. As Red was walking up to Matilda's house he noticed a cheery little sign welcoming him to the group. However, its constant smiling face and squeaky arms were just enough to send Red over the edge once again...

Inside, Red met his fellow classmates. Chuck, a superfast and enthusiastic yellow bird, Bomb who... well... has a problem with blowing up at the wrong time and Terence.

Matilda, a super-calm and friendly white bird, proceeded to show her class different ways of keeping their cool, including making art and writing poetry. Red did his best to try and avoid doing any of Matilda's tasks. In fact, he was trying so hard he almost didn't notice the commotion on the beach. Almost.

With the class dismissed, Red, Chuck and Bomb made their way to the crowd gathering around a strange ship – a ship that had managed to destroy Red's house as it landed on the beach.

No one had ever visited Bird Island before. As the gangplank lowered out stepped a strange, rather large and very green creature. **"Greetings!"** he said. **"I am a pig!"**

"What's a pig?" whispered Chuck.

15

BILLY IN BITS

Take a look at this picture of Billy before and after Red got angry with him. Try to spot the 6 differences in the 'after' shot.

A.

COULD THIS BE THE MOST ANNOYING SIGN OF ALL TIME?

BE HAPPY

SMILE

WELCOME ANGRY BIRDS

TODAY

B.

BE HAPPY

SMILE

WELCOME ANGRY BIRDS

SERENE SUDOKUS

Place each member of the Anger Management Class in each row, column and mini square once.

Colour in the squares!

Now try with the happy inhabitants of Bird Island!

17

WHAT HAS MADE RED ANGRY?

Follow the lines to see what is getting Red angrier than a pig at an empty buffet table.

A

B

BE HAPPY

SMILE

WELCOME ANGRY BIRDS

TODAY

C

D

Why so angry, Red?

18

MATILDA'S CLASS LIST

Matilda is just about to call the register for her latest Anger Management Class, but something looks wrong... Can you unscramble the names and match them to the right shadows?

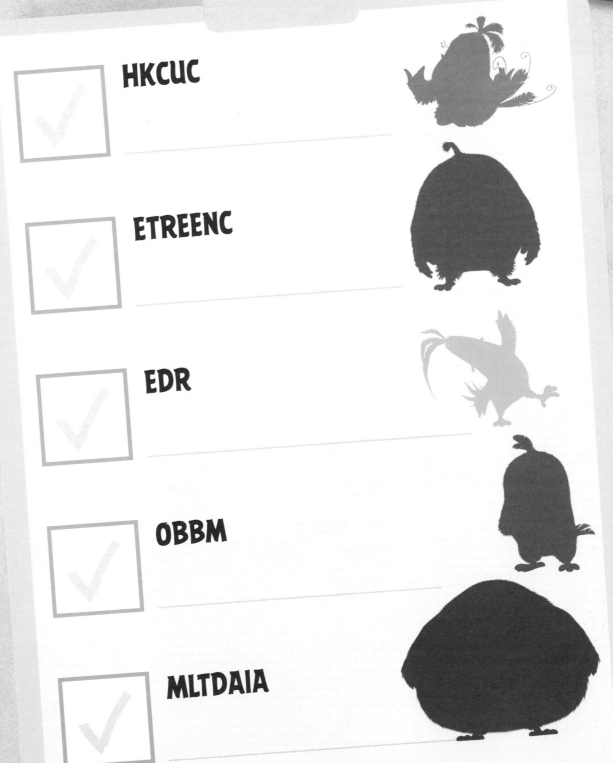

HKCUC

ETREENC

EDR

OBBM

MLTDAIA

19

GIANT WORDSEARCH

Can you find all the characters in the grid? Each name can go forwards, backwards, up, down and diagonally.

P	E	C	K	I	N	P	A	H	A	S	F	G
W	E	R	T	T	Y	U	H	G	C	V	M	K
Q	E	L	G	A	E	Y	T	H	G	I	M	J
X	Z	F	G	E	U	Y	H	J	I	O	K	L
A	T	L	E	O	N	A	R	D	C	W	E	H
D	E	D	F	V	B	N	H	J	Y	K	B	S
L	R	H	A	D	D	S	B	H	R	N	O	E
I	E	T	A	B	E	W	E	F	U	H	M	L
T	N	Q	W	L	E	R	R	T	S	Y	B	B
A	C	G	H	J	K	L	Z	X	C	V	B	B
M	E	W	E	D	F	T	C	H	U	C	K	U
S	D	W	S	T	E	L	L	A	E	R	F	B

Red　Peckinpah
Chuck　Stella
Bomb　Hal
Matilda　Bubbles
Mighty Eagle　Leonard
Cyrus　Terence

20

BOMB'S POEM

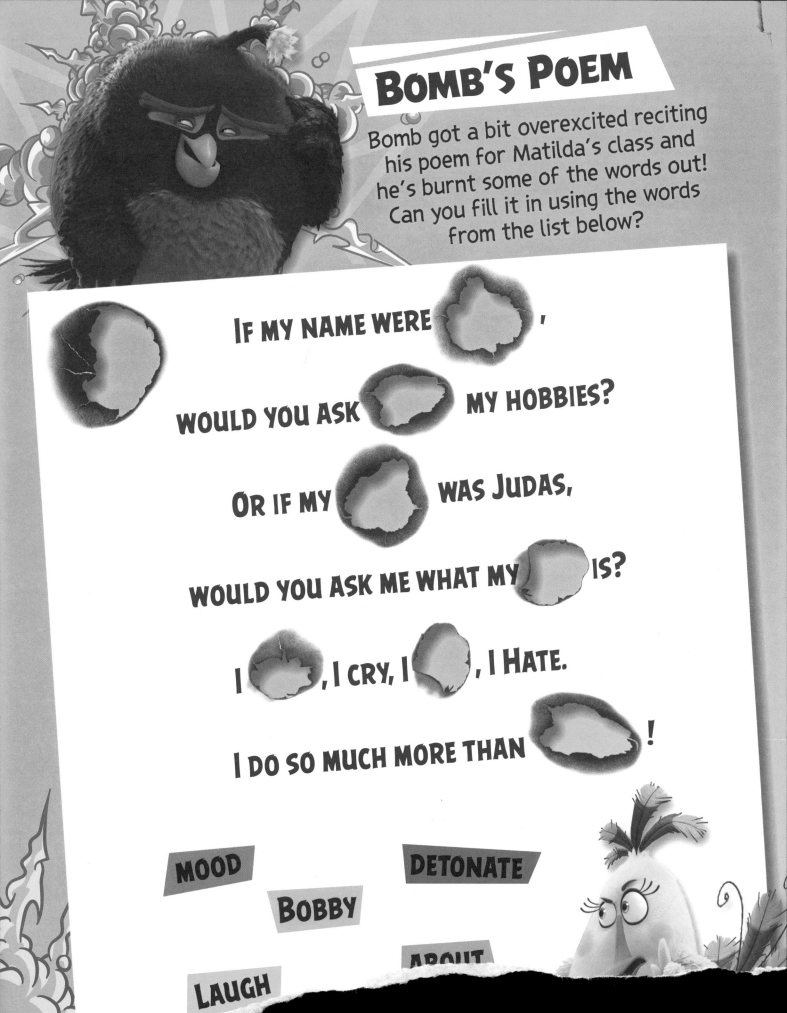

Bomb got a bit overexcited reciting his poem for Matilda's class and he's burnt some of the words out! Can you fill it in using the words from the list below?

IF MY NAME WERE ⬤ ,

WOULD YOU ASK ⬤ MY HOBBIES?

OR IF MY ⬤ WAS JUDAS,

WOULD YOU ASK ME WHAT MY ⬤ IS?

I ⬤ , I CRY, I ⬤ , I HATE.

I DO SO MUCH MORE THAN ⬤ !

MOOD

DETONATE

BOBBY

ABOUT

LAUGH

JUNGLE HIDE AND SEEK!

Bird Island is a beautiful tropical paradise – just look at all the luscious plants and flowers! Who can you see hiding amongst the jungle leaves?

CAN YOU FIND ALL THE ANGER MANAGEMENT CLASS MEMBERS HIDING IN THE JUNGLE PARADISE?

ANGRY BIRDS PART TWO:
We are the pigs!

No one really had a clue what these round, green, plucked creatures were, but they seemed friendly enough, so everyone welcomed them onto the island. Everyone, that is, apart from Red. There was just something about these round-bellied strangers that Red didn't trust...

While the two pigs made themselves at home, Red and the rest of the Anger Management Class went on with their sessions. Although Red was 100% sure he didn't need to be there, he had to admit he was enjoying hanging out with Chuck and Bomb.

normal as a ship can look to someone who's never been on one before. That was until the three feathered friends stumbled upon a secret room filled with more pigs!

Red immediately went to the rest of the birds to warn them that the pigs weren't as friendly as they were trying so hard to make out. But no one wanted to listen – after all, the pigs had just taught the birds how to fly using a giant slingshot. There was **NO WAY** these piggies were bad. Red was turned away.

The next day, however, the birds woke up to the most devastating news any bird could wish to hear. **THE EGGS WERE MISSING,** and guess who had taken them...?

You Crack Me Up!
Read these truly egg-cellent jokes!

Why did Judge Peckinpah sentence Red to Anger Management Classes?

Because he needed tweetment!

What do you call Chuck holding a sandwich?

Fast food!

Did you hear what happened when Bomb visited the nursery?

There was a real eggs-plosion!

Why were the baby birds sad?

They were feeling a little blue.

What do small birds learn in school?

Owlgebra

WHY DO HUMMINGBIRDS HUM?

BECAUSE THEY HAVE FORGOTTEN THE WORDS!

WHAT DO YOU CALL A CRATE OF DUCKS?

A BOX OF QUACKERS!

WHAT HAPPENED WHEN MIGHTY EAGLE FORGOT HOW TO FLY?

HE USED A SPARROW-CHUTE.

MATILDA DIDN'T WANT TO GO ON THE ROLLER COASTER, SHE WAS FEELING A LITTLE CHICKEN!

WHY IS A NEWSPAPER LIKE CHUCK'S BEST FRIEND?

BECAUSE THEY'RE BOTH 'RED' ALL OVER.

CALMING COLOURING

Feel totally Zen with Matilda's awesome colouring pages.

BIRD SNAPS

Can you work out who is in these Bird Snaps? Looks like someone needs to take a photography class.

1

2

3

Can you work out who is in these pictures?

31

FLYING FEATHERS

A few feathers must fly when birds get angry.
How many pairs of feathers
with matching patterns are there?
Some pairs are different colours.

ANGRY BIRDS PART THREE:
The birds strike back!

Chuck, Bomb and Red made their way to Mighty Eagle's cave, but when they arrived, they realised that Mighty Eagle wasn't the hero they thought he was. Red asked for help, but Mighty Eagle refused, he preferred to sit in his cave polishing trophies.

Just then, Red spotted a crowd of birds on their way to a party being held by the pigs. Underneath the stage at the party were huge piles of explosives!

Red, Chuck and Bomb raced back to the island, but it was too late. The pigs had stolen the eggs!

Judge Peckinpah turned to Red for help - after all, Red was the ONLY one who had guessed what the pigs were really up to. Red told the flock that they had to build a boat, get to Piggy Island and fight for their eggs!

On Pig Island, Red and the flock used the slingshot the pigs had shown them to launch themselves at the pigs' castle. It took a few goes, but soon the birds were flying through the air ready to get their eggs back.

Up on his mountain, Mighty Eagle watched as the drama unfolded beneath him. He shook off his feathers and took to the sky to help out.

With Red's cunning, the flock's crazy talents and Mighty Eagle, the birds managed to save their eggs and return to Bird Island.

With peace restored, the birds began to get back to life BP (before pigs). But not before they had given Red a gift they knew would make him the least angry he had ever been... They had rebuilt his house!

THE END

PLUMAGE PORTRAITS

Matilda has instructed the Anger Management group to paint self-portraits. Can you help?

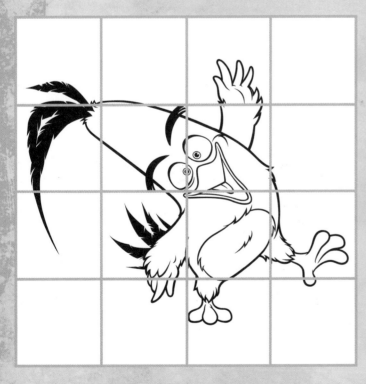

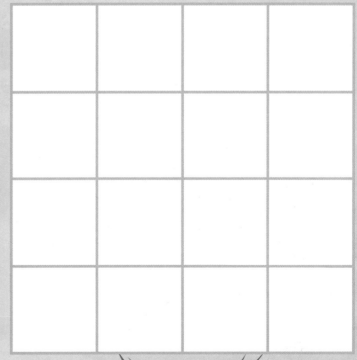

Copy the lines carefully!

CHUCK'S NEED FOR SPEED!

Ever wondered how Chuck stays so fast? **PRACTICE!**

WHAT YOU NEED TO DO:

1 Read Chuck's list of speedy tasks and have a go at each one.
2 When you are ready, set a timer and start the list of tasks.
3 Write down how long the whole list took to complete.
4 Now, start the tasks again and see if you can beat your time!

TASK LIST:

HOP ON ONE LEG THREE TIMES
LIE ON THE FLOOR
DO FOUR STAR JUMPS
SPIN ROUND TWICE

ROUND 1

ROUND 2

ROUND 3

ROUND 4

Will you be as speedy as Chuck?

COLOUR CHUCK!

Turn this page into a riot of colour, if you can pin Chuck down for long enough!

Be quick! Chuck won't hang around for long.

RIGHT SAID RED!

Red's beak can get him into trouble sometimes, but despite his bad temper he comes up with some pretty t-witty one-liners!

WHY DIDN'T YOU DO YOUR POEM?

WELL, YOU KNOW, I WAS GOING TO DO IT, BUT THEN I THOUGHT ABOUT IT AND I REALISED: "OH, THIS IS A HUGE WASTE OF MY TIME!" SO I DIDN'T DO IT.

THIS FEELS REALLY UNNATURAL...

HERE'S MY THOUGHT FOR THE DAY: WHEN ARE WE DONE?

CAN I JUST SAY, I NEVER UNDERSTAND A SINGLE THING YOU'RE TALKING ABOUT.

41

BOMB-TASTIC

Use your most explosive colours to colour in this picture of Bomb.

Calm down Bomb!

42

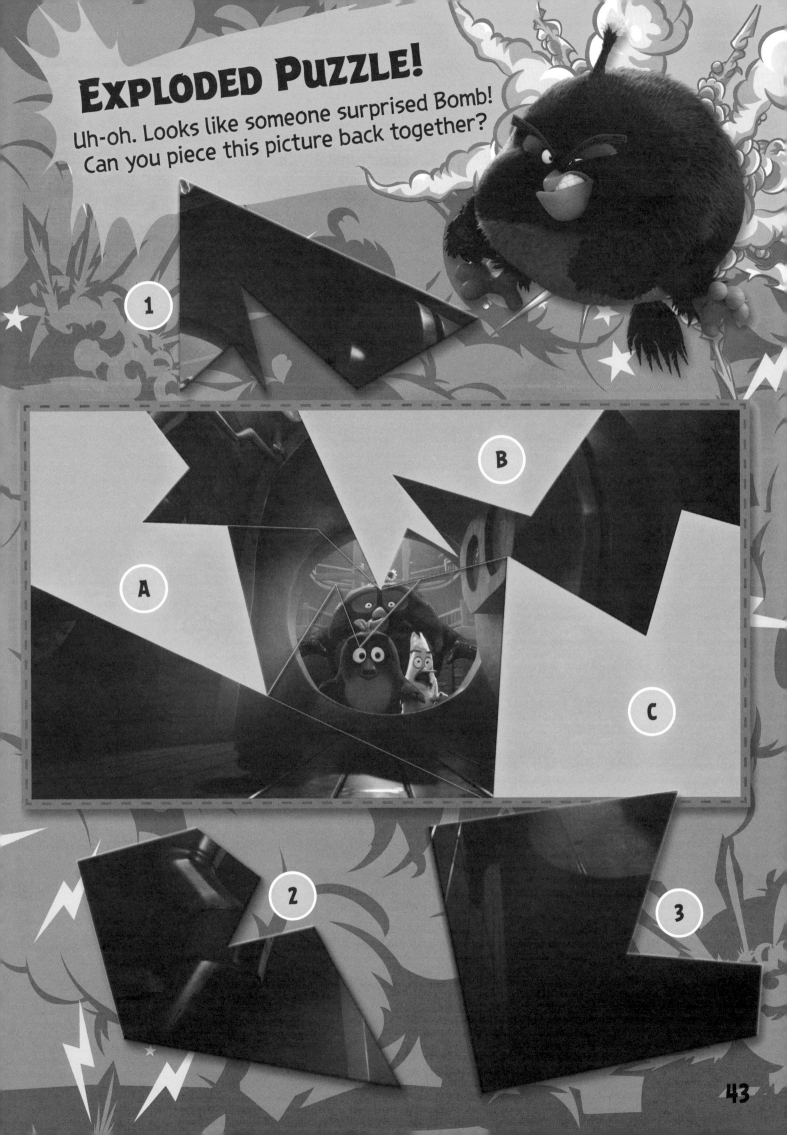

EXPLODED PUZZLE!

Uh-oh. Looks like someone surprised Bomb!
Can you piece this picture back together?

1

B

A

C

2

3

PIG PANDEMONIUM!

Can you sniff out all the piggy items on the list?

CAN YOU FIND:

6 UMBRELLAS
2 AEROPLANES
4 ICE CREAMS

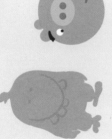

Add doodles to the pages!

45

MIGHTY EAGLE!

Use your most legendary colours to complete this heroic picture!

LEGEND

SPOT THE DIFFERENCE

The birds have found Mighty Eagle, and Chuck thinks it's a good time to take a photo! Can you see the four differences in the second picture?

BUILD A BOAT

Complete the grid to see if you are as good at building as the pigs!

M
A
i S L A N d
n
r E d
e
F m
L e
o A n G
c t
t

EGGS   ANGER   MANAGEMENT

FLOCK   RED   ISLAND

AHOY THERE, PIG!

Now try going from Red to Pig!

WORK YOUR WAY DOWN THE LADDER, CHANGING *ONLY* ONE LETTER TO MAKE A NEW WORD EACH TIME.

CAN YOU GET FROM SHIP TO SAIL IN FOUR STEPS?

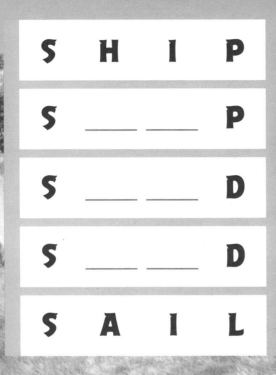

S	H	I	P
S	___	___	P
S	___	___	D
S	___	___	D
S	A	I	L

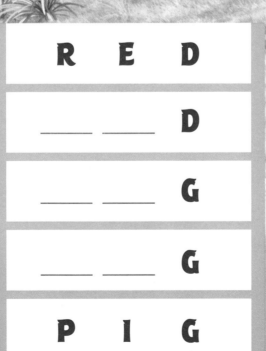

R	E	D
___	___	D
___	___	G
___	___	G
P	I	G

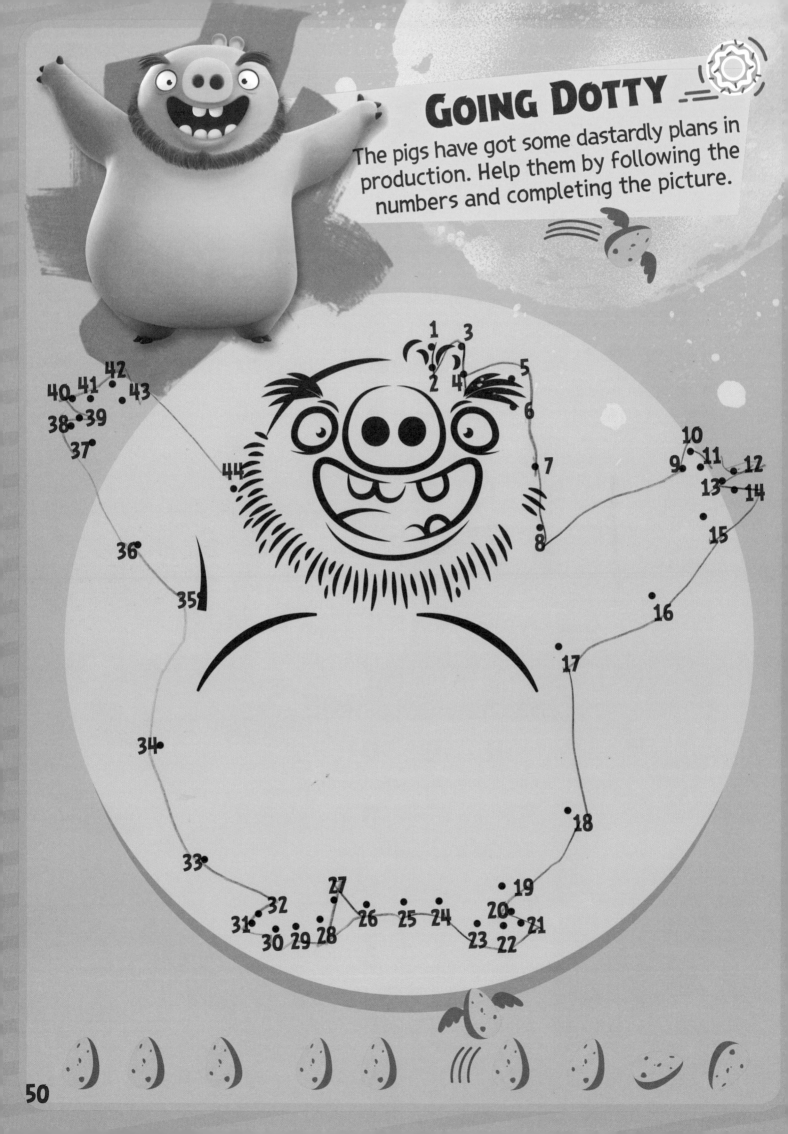

GOING DOTTY

The pigs have got some dastardly plans in production. Help them by following the numbers and completing the picture.

SCRAMBLED LINES

A poor egg has been left unattended! But who's going to get to it first?

A

B

C

GET THE EGGS!

Help the flock reach Bird Island with as many eggs as possible!

START

2

3
Great start! You've found 1 egg.

4
Uh-oh. You drop an egg into Leonard's lap – lose an egg.

5

6

7
Quick! Collect 2 eggs before one of the pigs sees you.

12
Collect 1 egg from a sleeping pig.

13

14
Find a shortcut! Go forward 2 spaces.

15

20
Bomb's exploded! Go back 1 space.

21

22
Oh no! Leonard is in your way. Lose 2 eggs.

23
Nearly there! Collect 1 egg.

HOW TO PLAY:

1 Cut out or copy the playing pieces and the 20 eggs.
2 Give each player 3 eggs.
3 Take it in turns to roll a die and move around the board.
4 Whoever reaches Bird Island with the most eggs is the **WINNER!** If you lose all your eggs before the end of the game, the other player **WINS**.

8

9
Get distracted by Mighty Eagle and lose 2 eggs.

10
Go back 2 spaces to find Terence.

11

16

17
Lose an egg overboard!

18
Collect an egg from a secret piggy stash.

19

24

FINISH
Bird Island!
You made it!

GET TO PIGGY ISLAND!

Red is leading the birds to rescue the eggs!
Can you help him? Watch out
for any pigs along the way!

START

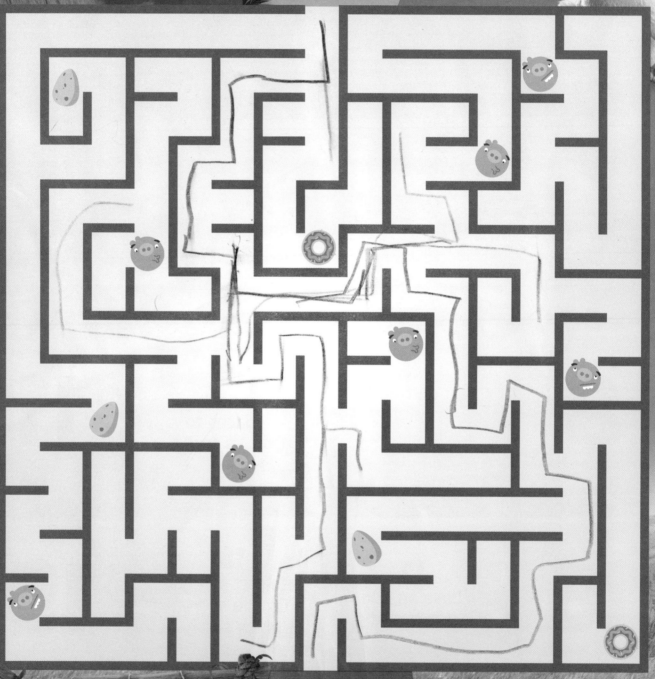

FINISH

Do the maze
again and get
to each egg!

PIG PERFECTION

The Pigs love order. Arrange these piggy followers so that there is only one of each in every row, column and mini square.

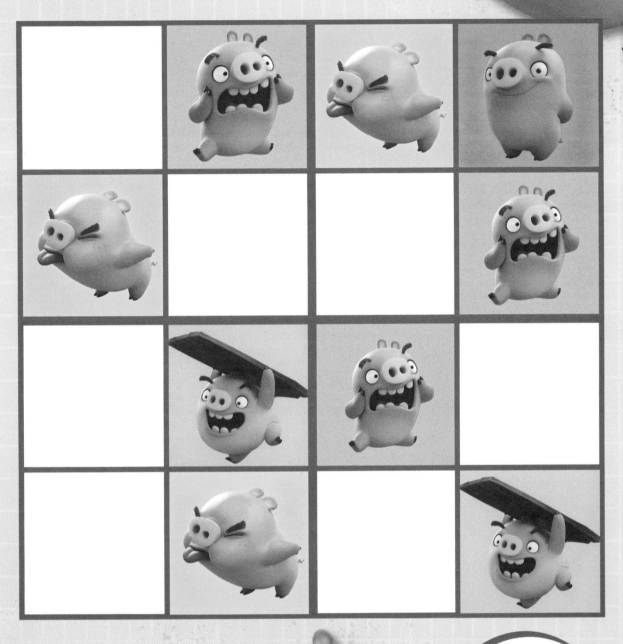

Colour in the squares to complete the puzzle!

THE BIG FAT ANGRY QUIZ!

If you think you know everything there is to know about the Angry Birds and their foes, see if you can ace this test!

1 WHAT IS RED SENT TO ANGER MANAGEMENT LESSONS FOR?

....

2 NAME THE FOUR BIRDS IN MATILDA'S ANGER MANAGEMENT CLASS.

....

3 WHAT'S THE NAME OF CHUCK'S BELOVED SIGN?

....

4 WHERE DOES RED LIVE?

....

5 WHO DOES TERENCE HAVE A SECRET CRUSH ON?

....

6 WHO DOES JUDGE PECKINPAH USE TO MAKE HIM BIGGER?

....

7 HOW MANY PIGS DOES LEONARD SAY ARE ON THE BOAT?

....

56

8 WHERE DO RED, CHUCK AND BOMB FIND THE REST OF THE PIGS HIDING?

....

9 WHAT'S THE NAME OF THE BIRD WITH PINK PLUMAGE?

....

....

10 WHAT IS THE ONE THING MIGHTY EAGLE IS SUPPOSED TO BE ABLE TO DO THAT THE REST OF THE BIRDS CAN'T?

....

....

11 WHAT'S MATILDA'S SPECIAL TALENT?

....

12 WHERE DOES MIGHTY EAGLE LIVE?

....

13 WHAT DO THE PIGS TEACH THE BIRDS TO DO?

....

14 WHAT DO THE PIGS WANT WITH ALL THE EGGS?

....

15 WHAT CRUSHES RED'S HOUSE?

....

SNORTING CHORTLES

WHAT IS THE PIGS' BOAT MADE OF?

MaHOGany!

WHAT HAPPENED WHEN THE PIG PEN BROKE?

THEY HAD TO USE A PENCIL INSTEAD!

WHAT DO YOU GET WHEN YOU CROSS A PIG WITH A CACTUS?

A PORK-UPINE!

WHAT HAPPENED TO LEONARD WHEN RED STOLE THE EGGS BACK?

HE TURNED GREEN WITH ENVY!

WHAT DID THE MUMMY PIG SAY TO THE FRIGHTENED BABY PIG?

DON'T WORRY, IT'S JUST A PIGMENT OF YOUR IMAGINATION.

WHAT DO THE PIGS USE WHEN THEY ARE POORLY?

OINKMENT

WHAT DID JUDGE PECKINPAH LIKE ABOUT THE PIGS?

HE THOUGHT THEY WERE QUITE STY-LISH.

ANSWERS

P16 Billy in Bits

P17 Serene Sudokus

P18 What Has Made Red Angry?
Answer: B

P19 Matilda's Class List

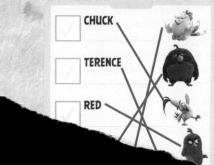

P20 Giant Wordsearch

P21 Bomb's Poem
If my name were *Bobby*, would you ask *about* my hobbies?
Or if my *name* was Judas, would you ask me what my *mood* is?
I *laugh*, I cry, I *love*, I hate.
I do so much more than *detonate*!

P22-23 Jungle Hide and Seek

P30-31 Bird Snaps
1 Chuck, 2 Terence, 3 Stella,
4 Mighty Eagle, 5 Red, 6 Bomb

P32-33 Flying Feathers
There are 9 pairs of feathers

P43 Exploded Puzzle!
A 2, B 1, C 3

P44-45 Pig Pandemonium!

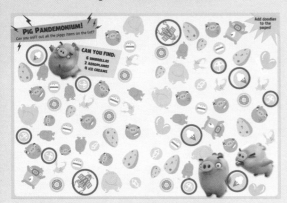

P47 Spot The Difference

P48 Build a Boat

P49 Ahoy There, Pig!

S	H	I	P
S	L	I	P
S	L	I	D
S	A	I	D
S	A	I	L

R	E	D
B	E	D
B	E	G
B	I	G

P51 Scrambled Lines
Answer: B

P54 Get To Piggy Island!

P55 Pig Perfection

P56-57 The Big Fat Angry Quiz!
1 Causing chaos at young hatchling's party
2 Red, Chuck, Bomb and Terence
3 Billy
4 On the beach
5 Matilda
6 Cyrus
7 Two
8 On the boat
9 Stella
10 Fly
11 Staying calm at all times
12 In a cave on the mountaintop
13 Fly